Emily's Advice to Girls in the New Millennium

poems by

Rosemarie Dombrowski

Finishing Line Press
Georgetown, Kentucky

Emily's Advice to Girls in the New Millennium

Copyright © 2025 by Rosemarie Dombrowski
ISBN 979-8-89990-166-9 First Edition
All rights reserved under International and Pan-American Copyright Conventions. No part of this book may be reproduced in any manner whatsoever without written permission from the publisher, except in the case of brief quotations embodied in critical articles and reviews.

ACKNOWLEDGMENTS

Sixthly, Ninthly, Eleventhly, Twelfthly, Nineteenthly, and *Twenty-Eighthly* appeared in the *Digging Through the Fat*, April 2021.

Secondly, Thirteenthly, Seventeenthly, Thirty-Firstly, Thirty-Fifthly, Thirty-Eighthly, Unbound sheets 40-50, and *Unbound sheets 51-75* appeared in *A Dozen Nothing*, October 2021.

ABOUT THE COVER ARTIST

Letisia Cruz is a Cuban-American writer and artist. She is the author of *Bigwig's Illustrated Guide To Birds* (Tolsun Books, 2024), *Migrations & Other Exiles* (Lost Horse Press, 2023), selected by Dzvinia Orlowsky as winner of the 2022 Idaho Prize for Poetry, and *The Lost Girls Book of Divination* (Tolsun Books, 2018). She is the recipient of a 2022 artist grant from the St. Petersburg Arts Alliance and was selected as a 2022 Dali Dozen Emerging Artist for her project Rituales: An Exploration of Faith in the Caribbean. Her writing and art-work have appeared in [PANK], *Ninth Letter, The Acentos Review, Gulf Stream, Saw Palm, Third Coast, Duende, Moko, 300 Days of Sun,* and *Black Fox Literary Magazine,* among others. She is a graduate of Fairleigh Dickinson University's MFA program and lives in Saint Peters-burg, Florida with her partner and their three cats.

Publisher: Leah Huete de Maines
Editor: Christen Kincaid
Cover Art: Letisia Cruz

Cover Design: Elizabeth Maines McCleavy

Order online: www.finishinglinepress.com
also available on amazon.com

Author inquiries and mail orders:
Finishing Line Press
PO Box 1626
Georgetown, Kentucky 40324
USA

For all the women (and girls) who have strengthened my resolve, fostered my creativity, and helped me realize my potential.

The Twine that Binds: A Note on Emily Dickinson's Fascicles (Zines) & the Poems

When Emily Dickinson's 40 hand-written, hand-bound books—aka zines—were found after her death, Mabel Loomis Todd (Emily's brother's mistress) gave them the name *fascicles*.

After decades of neglect and deconstruction at the hands of male scholars and editors, the fascicles were eventually restored and reprinted by Cristanne Miller in *Emily Dickinson's Poems: As She Preserved Them* (2016), a mere 120 years after Emily's death.

Upon reading the restored fascicles/zines, I realized that each one is a manifesto or confession, an act of rebellion or erotica, an advice column on life, love, and death. The themes of Emily D.'s fascicles make the connections easy to see, especially when you're a product (and scholar) of the riot grrrl revolution—Emily D. is our zinester foremother.

And in true zinester fashion, the poems in this collection are loose translations of the fascicles/zines, cut-ups born out of borrowed phrases and stolen ideas. They are one possible version of the advice that Emily D. coded into her pages and bound with twine—advice born out of some of the earliest DIY poetry zines in America.

The Fascicles

First

Every couplet is a mysterious prayer, a pilgrimage into a thorny patch of mind. Remember what you've forgotten—that the moral is painted in ballads and love songs. That the mourning is choked in sand. Recite the names of the constellations and their meanings. Sleep beneath a tree. You can never separate yourself from the waters of grief, and you will never row to shore. Loss is the deepest hallelujah, so spread your wings and sigh.

Second

How syllables can pierce the body. How songs can be tarnished. How you bless the soldiers and count their feet. When the woods have been robbed and the wheels spun, pray to the god of forgetfulness—deep within the bark. When your heart is a violet buried in snow. When you've searched the forest for weapons and only found words. How there's a quietness without birds, no offerings murmuring the names of roses.

Third

There are elegies struggling to breathe, petals buried in gold, grief that can't take flight. Measure the distance between the snake and the angels that you pluck from the garden. Who gets delayed—the dignity of the body or the carriage of death? Like the morning dew, time gurgles on. Hide yourself in a flower. Dive deep within the soil. Philosophy is less believable than the poverty of loss.

Fourth

When you're heavy-hearted. When you're hazardous to yourself. Climb into the nest that you came from and wrap yourself in grace. When they raffle your soul. When they stun you with winter winds. The daisies and daffodils will survive it. The thirsty flower can be fed by the brook like Jesus can resurrect the dead, so cast your ballot, and bear witness with the quiet eyes of a saint.

Fifth

Let your eyes settle into the caravan of a summer night—a mist of madness, the bells hovering like a softly plucked morning. The bees have gone mad and the soldiers have been defeated again. When the night is both fading and glowing. When the ecstasy expires. When the twigs snap under your feet like the feathery perfume of death. Picture the features of her face in the quivering sunrise and jostle yourself awake.

Sixth

You are always emerging from your cocoon, watching the levels of water in the creek—barefooted and breezy. Drink the wine that grows the seeds of the world. How the answers can be found in the woods. How the return of the birds is a sacrament. How commerce won't stop when you die. When you lose a friend in childhood, it will tear you apart as many times as you're able to sew yourself back up again—because life is chaos and the world is synesthesia and someday, you won't be able to tell morning from night.

Seventh

The anatomy of silence. The non-speaking hours. Bones tagged and catalogued like saints. Theories of flora pressed into a book. There is more loss than you can bury in the garden, and though the weeds will over-take you, they will never tell you what to believe. The ghosts trapped in a field of poppies, the gymnastics of the body licking its own wounds.

Eighth

When the horses trample the garden. When the angels circle their wagons. When the little spirits hide in the grasses. The joy of your breath will keep you from dying of thirst. Gallop until the wounds split open, until the pain pollinates the spring, bribes it with roses scattered across the lawn like a smokescreen.

Ninth

When the narrative has failed and the body is a tempest—the cool forehead and the closed mouth. The dull flies buzzing around the river, gracious and weeping. The music of the sky like witchcraft. Who keeps your secrets? Who gets the credit? Can your eyes see beyond the veil? When your heart is a church, you can believe whatever you want about the afterlife.

Tenth

Get drunk on nectar. Place your head in the cup—all the way inside it, until you can see angels playing in the distance, until you're touching yourself in the morning, a new light burning inside you, so much fire. How do I say this—there's going to be agony. But there will be roses in the desert, maybe a trail of crumbs leading into the garden of Eden. When the sea dissolves into midnight, ask the sparrow for forgiveness. Say *I have nothing else to bring you, and I don't know the way home.*

Eleventh

When the monarchy stops making sense. When you're nothing more than a drop in the sea. When the dazzling things disappear in the night. The way anonymity can give you freedom, the freaks in their death masks worshipping the stars. When you're called to suffer, when you're called to grieve. When you puzzle your way through the lexicon of June. When you pray for the freedom to be wild, to row away from the shores of convention like the heroine of a folk song.

Twelfth

Try to find something else to get high on—maybe the banquet of summer. When the drunken messages come too quickly, when the kingdom snaps in half and the ghosts fall like acorns. When the names become sensations and grace is carried away by the breeze. When the order of the words doesn't make sense, there's a network of veins just under the surface of the page, chirping like crickets, and that's the language that you may not be able to translate, so you just have to feel something.

Thirteenth

When there's a train ravaging the woods behind your house. When there's a pool of grief settling beneath the tree. Read the history of rebellion until you understand what they were fighting, until you're less afraid than you were before. The best crucifix is one that fits in your pocket, like an invisible belief. There's no such thing as magic—just a door to a room filled with birds, the sound of your heartbeat extinguished.

Fourteenth

The perfume of madness and the apple tree, how they tease you like a dream. When your breath can't be controlled. When the philosophy of life becomes accident-prone. Stab the bird and kill your balm. Burst through the gate and escape. Drop your life into the mystic well and release your blame—the earth lays down under a skein of misery.

Fifteenth

The sentences are clocks, and the strings snap like madness—the mumblings of your brain predicted by science. The moon is eclipsed. Your eyes are hungry for light, but the color of the grave is darkness. The shame of a sentence, the leaves murmuring with hunger—the feelings you can't articulate.

Sixteenth

Don't ignore the throbbing in your head, the angle of light as it enters the eye. The truth is a ghostly vision and the sweetness of fruit is invisible. When the trees go deaf. When the road plunges into your chest, the horses breaking free of their harnesses. When you start to know things, the cold will seep into your bones and you'll be finished knowing.

Seventeenth

When bees stop pollinating and things stop growing. When you become unrecognizable to yourself. When you finally make love again. When you start believing in the afterlife. When the flies are hovering above the water, landing on the rinds that you've tossed in the grass. The act of baptizing yourself is the only one that counts—

Eighteenth

When pain is an earthquake knocking at your chest. When your memory begins to lose itself. Pray for the lives of other species. Pray for the grace of Mozart to enter your body like an act of God. Let the saints lead you into the sea. Let your brain taste every spice. Let it sing like the ripest rose on the bush.

Nineteenth

Like a midnight girl in a daytime town. Like the odors of girlhood. How you dance your way through the mortus of the brain, the clutching and groping of goblins drinking dew. Death is another way of forgetting Jesus. Girls should never be separated in childhood, which is another way of saying you'd cross the Baltic sea for her—that angel, this lullaby.

Twentieth

The dust measured by the dram. The haunting in your head. A train breaking through like little notes of bird-song. Nothing can prepare you for the weight of the afternoon, the white heat of evening. Who's to say what's divine—maybe the surgeon and the angel, the revolver under your bed and the door that you bolt behind you.

Twenty-first

When you're years from home, when you're facing the danger—veiled love or a fork in the road. When you've lived small and confined, trapped in the prose of life until your brain explodes like a star. Latch it with your hand. The wooden laugh, the sinking rose given to you by the gods. No matter what you do, advance the journey. Feel your way around the bowels of language and fly.

Twenty-second

Stop obsessing over the blades and the final blow. The seasons are emotions, like a beach filled with pearls, a red-eyed orchard brimming with magic—the geography of the afterlife, untraceable with your finger, the electricity of the soul. Dwell on the possibilities then nap for a century.

Twenty-third

When your house is sinking. When you're riding into the sunset for the last time. When you have so little to lose. Mute your mind and find the blessings in a crumb. When there's a different kind of blankness, there's a different kind of story. When you undress yourself in the hills. When you listen to the winds of recollection. Don't ignore the dread that you're desperate to pray away.

Twenty-fourth

God is a man and hell is a bomb that he created, a battle between boyhood desires. How could you possibly know that atoms could be split? How could you solve the unsolvable equations? None of it is your fault, and even if you could stop it, no one would give you a medal. Maybe the bravery of confession is the only liberty.

Twenty-fifth

The moment before the wreck is fear. The moment after is despair. There are two butterflies in the garden, imaginary chariots racing eternity to the grave, the winds teasing us like Sappho. The soul lashed by fire. The flood you try to hide in a drawer. Lift the lid and ask the heart what pleasure is, but only if you're ready for the answer.

Twenty-sixth

You know what it means when the flies are buzzing, when serpents and ghosts invade your thoughts like lightning, when your soul disengages and your head slides away. Remember the summer, when the future shone like pearls and your brain was bigger than the sky. Before you write your final poem, the bells will toll, the night sky will spark violets, and you'll know that you're still alive when you hear the robin singing in your head, unable to tell grief from joy.

Twenty-seventh

When there's a death in the opposite house—the language of drowsiness, the body losing its vitality, the dark parade a kind of medicine for the aching soul. Measuring grief is harder than you think. Bravery comes in the strangest forms of summer—a blackberry, a single hair, a sunset in a sonnet. Fate is easier to navigate when you know what to carry and what to leave behind. How few the beautiful moments when you live in stupor—that should be punishment enough

Twenty-eighth

When there's nothing left but the parable of the dying tiger, or Jesus hanging like stalactites from the cross. When there's nothing but paragraphs holding the dying, the alphabet spelling winter, its loneliness and failure, boys saluting and never returning home. When you awaken from an illness of mind and you don't know what to believe. When the petals drop and your body tremors, imagine a carnival of clouds, a mythic woman comforting you as you sob on her shoulder. When you pray for something silly, you can be sure that no one's listening.

Twenty-ninth

A woman tucked inside a butterfly. An allusion to frost in a dream—golden spider, the carbon in the coal. How could God be your lover when you're trapped in domesticity? The mouth of the cavern you stood in, the way madness can be divine, the earth simulating your thoughts in the form of prayer. Say it one more time and savor it—Divine Insanity.

Thirtieth

Beauty can be found in the creases—creatures emerging from the sea, roses in their mouths. When the golden dawn becomes the apocalypse, you will have fewer reasons to be awake, but you will make art, and you will want to be martyred for it—the nobility shamed, their ignorance confirmed, the unrecorded suffering of heretics.

Thirty-first

When your heart blisters and the river can't reach you. When you can see the sky from the inside. Clutch it with your eye like notes in the margins—a sip of wine, a slice of future mind. When it strikes you like a storm or when you're dying in the eye of it. When death comes three times. When the heavens are stitched shut, you decay on the other side.

Thirty-second

Stop wasting your pages on lifeless lovers. Stop looking death in the face—you're not that brave, but you have *the power to be true to You*. Host prayers, sew a button. Repeat the supplication until you absorb it. When you're fumbling at midnight. When the needle and thread become useless. When you're awakened by the dream where you lose your teeth or die from a staggering blow. How suffering is like kindling—

Thirty-third

Bury yourself with the stiff, cold letters you've written in secret. Ink your pain onto the page and Jesus will stare back at you with wide-eyed kindness. Dream of squirrels and the crucifixion, poisonous berries and other modest needs. If you're separated at sea, ask her to explain the legacy of love, to show you its capaciousness.

Thirty-fourth

You think about what it means to live. You think about the days. The pain eventually blanks your mind. You picture a sweet, nostalgic homestead, the illegitimate summer, how it poured into you like bliss. No matter how long the road, the grave is always waiting with a loaded gun.

Thirty-fifth

When it's dusk, and your feet are drowsy from collecting shells along the coast. When you cut off the tip of your ear and your spirit becomes audible. When you realize the years have begun to crack. When you start calculating the convergences. If the owl is our judge and there is no heaven, what's the purpose of all this? Glaciers, the muteness in the house, divine love—things that are out of sight. The peace rollicking at sea. A balloon is simply a metaphor for life.

Thirty-sixth

No one can invent this—a troubling ache, a haunted decade. When you listen, your mother sends messages in the shape of a cricket's song. You are prisoner, apparition, wayward woman of god. You break loaves and multiply crumbs. You'd trade your kingdom for a miracle. No one can steal your tongue or refuse your syllables. No one can crack your shell. Good night, zephyr, good night, sweet Madonna. The ocean polishes your heart like a diamond.

Thirty-seventh

Not the particles that connect you. Not a solitary acre. Not the theater of the heart. Suspense and remorse. Death and the bitter Juliet. The grace of birds. How you bloom things without names. How they auction your mind one fascicle at a time. Maybe you're not worthy. Maybe you've been accused. Sometimes, fate sinks you like a stone.

Thirty-eighth

The final drop of summer. Necklaces made of breeze. How the brook swallows the dust and gives the blind their sight. The port-less window. The split sky. The disadvantage of despair.
How the circumference and diameter can never be equivalent. No message, no remedy, no satiation—the bleakness that time can never heal.

Thirty-ninth

When you're starved for love. When your god has been arrested. Fling yourself into the night and become the oldest oak, the 4pm song and the 6pm flood. When you can no longer taste it. When the glittering has been eclipsed by the weary. When nothing can appease it, the misery like sinew, that's when you'll feel it—wind, death, pleasure, though not necessarily in that order.

Fortieth

I have news for you about eternity—it's stranger than you can imagine, like an ungracious country, a tribunal conviction, a Midsummer death and a brutal birth. Sometimes, even the most esteemed ideas can't protect us, but light enables light, convex and concave, the necessary angles of God. Pain is another way of saying *conundrum of time*. When Death stretches its long, democratic fingers. When a crescent moon fills the sky. When the big calamity strikes, revolution is on the horizon.

The Unbound Sheets

P.S.

When there are monsters in your heart, when midnight repeats itself—let the taste of it hover like the sunset. Touch the full breast of the moon with your tongue. When you become confused, when you forget the secrets, when you're struck by love or the forces of nature without conclusion. Before your eyesight starts to fail, before your mind splits apart, before the flash of danger overtakes you, conjure what you need to remember.

P.S.S.

When everything is disembodied. When it all becomes a mirage. Split the lark like a struggling mind, a blameless experiment in delight. Let your words create sparks, your discourse burn like fire. A woman is a bird, an undiscovered continent, a plank hovering precariously over the sea. A poet is a rose, a wick, a final horizon, the language of crickets that we can only decipher when the waters begin to close above our head. You never know when the doom will overtake you, so count your scars and drink up.

P.S.S.S.

When you have witnessed too many winters—the firing squad and the arrow through the heart, the armies warring outside your door. The truth lies in topography, the bridge of faith that we jump from. The map of the astronomer is the compass of the sailor. When your cataracts begin conjugating like verbs, transforming from a solid to a liquid. If only you could feel God in your body, like bells frantically ringing, a rose blooming in Sicily. The philosophy of ruin is a slow dialogue, so begin by counting all the syllables in all the poems you've ever written.

P.S.S.S.S.

You are neither the bird in the hand nor the one in the bush—maybe a thick crust of dust, a chemical conviction, the atoms in a strand of hair. Life is a dragon's claw—the trifling and the dying repeated over and over again, the bliss that can never eclipse it. According to your zodiac, Revolution is in bloom. Hinge your days with acquaintances and art, water and nutrition, maybe a velvet cheek at midnight, a lover with tentacles like the clover's root.

P.S.S.S.S.S.

Not the days anchored by divinity. Not the condemned lip or the fissure in the moon, the tissues stuffed under the door. The famine of vanity and the foreignness of your own face—like an immigrant without a settlement, the hollows of your eyes like the house we can never inhabit together. The crisis behind the door. The habits we form out of curiosity. How we become pioneers of disaster. How we have accepted the chemical concoction of fate. How we have witnessed the conviction of atoms. To be impaled is to have a liturgy composed in your honor, like little gifts of meat hanging from the trees, the squirrels singing your name as they devour the bloody hearts.

P.S.S.S.S.S.

Like a witch, she's carved a breathing woman out of corn, dropped your brain in the deepest water, her lips a scarlet buzz. The doors are closing and you can feel it—like the end of a June exhibition, like your mind italicized, the aloneness in the room like a single blade of grass, like the way an idea is like a door without a caption, a wrinkled morning and a nameless bird, the bread you store for later, the decade flying by like a circus, the seeds destroyed, everything outgrowing itself as the girls sigh their stupid sighs and wave goodbye.

P.S.S.S.S.S.S.

Maybe a woman is a shivering leaf, a one-eyed whip, an antique bird yellowing like bone, a creature of the night, the crickets singing like a heartbeat, her cocoon tightening like a memory without syllables, like tonguing a book filled with blossoms, a bed filled with flowers, the wilderness that ceases to breathe you, the awful beauty of the funeral of god, how she wears a crown of grass around her brain in memorium, how she becomes the queen of the subterranean cellar of the soul.

Rosemarie Dombrowski (RD) is the inaugural Poet Laureate of Phoenix, AZ, the founding editor of rinky dink press, and the founding director of Revisionary Arts, a nonprofit that facilitates self-care and healing through poetry. She is the recipient of an Arts Hero Award, a Great 48 award, a Laureate Fellowship from the Academy of American Poets, an Arizona Humanities Speaker of the Year award, and an Arizona Capital Times Leader of the Year award.

RD has published three collections of poetry: *The Book of Emergencies* (Five Oaks Press, 2014), *The Philosophy of Unclean Things* (Finishing Line Press, 2017), and *The Cleavage Planes of Southwest Minerals [A Love Story]*, winner of the 2017 Split Rock Review chapbook competition. She was named a finalist for both the Whitman Bicentennial Award (2019) and the Joy Harjo Poetry Contest (2023), and her work has been featured on the TEDx stage, NPR, and in numerous publications.

RD is a Teaching Professor at Arizona State University specializing in medical poetry, the poetry of witness, and DIY print culture. She is the founding faculty editor of *ISSUED: stories of service*, the creator of Verses for Vets, and the faculty editor of *Grey Matter*, the medical poetry journal at the University of Arizona College of Medicine-Phoenix.

She lives in Phoenix with her son (B) and her three cats (PB&J).

www.ingramcontent.com/pod-product-compliance
Lightning Source LLC
Chambersburg PA
CBHW030059170426
43197CB00010B/1594